W9-BCT-075

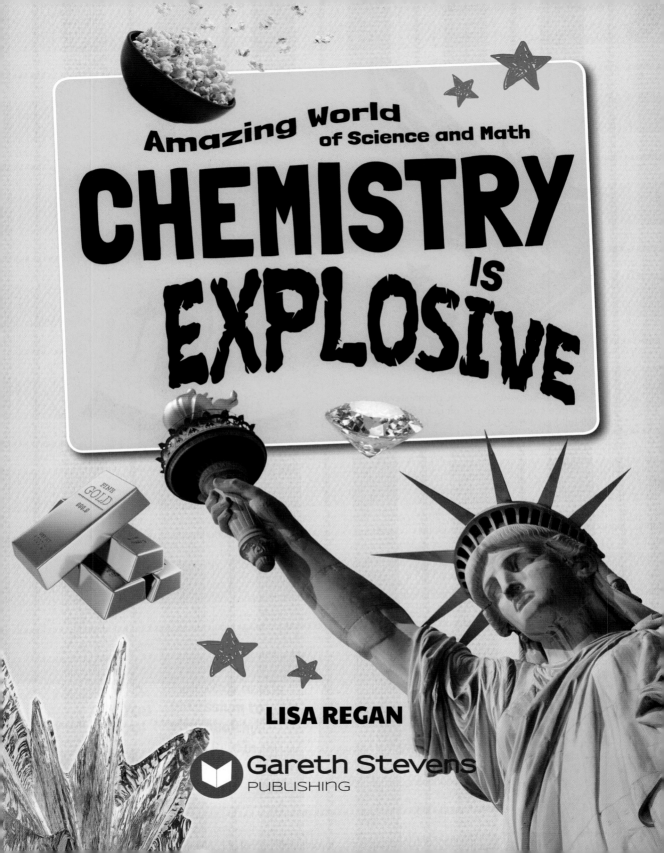

Amazing World of Science and Math

CHEMISTRY IS EXPLOSIVE

LISA REGAN

Gareth Stevens
PUBLISHING

Please visit our website, www.garethstevens.com.
For a free color catalog of all our high-quality books,
call toll free 1-800-542-2595 or fax 1-877-542-2596.

Cataloging-in-Publication Data

Names: Regan, Lisa.
Title: Chemistry is explosive / Lisa Regan.
Description: New York : Gareth Stevens Publishing, 2017. | Series: Amazing world of science
   and math | Includes index.
Identifiers: ISBN 9781482449907 (pbk.) | ISBN 9781482449921 (library bound) |
   ISBN 9781482449914 (6 pack)
Subjects: LCSH: Chemistry–Juvenile literature.
Classification: LCC QD35.R44 2017 | DDC 540–dc23

Published in 2017 by
Gareth Stevens Publishing
111 East 14th Street, Suite 349
New York, NY 10003

All images from Shutterstock except p5 Nasa; p7(t) aphotostory/Shutterstock.com;
p25 Wellcome Library; p35 (t) Gilles Paire/Shutterstock.com; p39(b) Wellcome Library

Printed in the United States of America
CPSIA compliance information: Batch CS16GS:
For further information contact Gareth Stevens, New York, New York at 1-800-542-2595.

Contents

THE STATUE OF LIBERTY USED TO BE ORANGE

Chemistry doesn't just happen in labs. It's all around us! It's the reason the sun shines, what makes your cake rise, and it's also the reason why the Statue of Liberty has gradually turned green. All of those things are CHEMICAL REACTIONS.

A green goddess

Presented to the United States as a gift in 1886, this world-famous statue didn't always look the way it does today. The framework is made of iron, but the statue is covered on the outside with a thin layer of copper. Copper is a metal that gradually turns green as it reacts with the air; this chemical reaction is called **patination**. It actually helps to protect the statue from the weather and stop it from falling apart.

Getting a reaction

A chemical reaction changes one substance into a different substance. It cannot be reversed. Lighting a candle starts a reaction called **combustion**. The burning candle wax reacts with oxygen in the air to give off heat and light. New substances are formed such as smoke, steam, and carbon dioxide gas.

Why is my bike rusty?

When iron and steel come into contact with water and oxygen, they oxidize, making a new substance called rust. Water and oxygen are both found in the atmosphere, and even more water is added to the situation if you leave your bike out in the rain! Rusting is an example of **corrosion**. Painting the metal helps to protect it from rusting by sealing it against the corrosive substances.

Did You Know

A rusty bicycle weighs the same as the original bike, even though it looks different.

Everyday occurrence

It's not only scientists who do science. If you bake a cake, you are using a series of chemical changes to produce something yummy. Striking a match, washing your hair, and using bug repellent are all examples of chemistry taking place.

Body basics

Your body is a giant laboratory with lots of chemistry experiments going on all the time. When you eat, your body uses chemical reactions to turn the food into energy. When you breathe, you take in air and use the oxygen to fuel your body's cells. During the process, a waste gas called carbon dioxide is produced. Even a scab forming on a cut is an example of a chemical process.

Did You Know

Mars is called the Red Planet because its surface is covered in red iron oxide, or rust.

THE STUDY OF CHEMICAL REACTIONS IN LIVING THINGS IS CALLED BIOCHEMISTRY.

ANTARCTIC SNOW DOESN'T MAKE SNOWBALLS

Snow needs to be slightly wet to squish and stick into snowballs, but Antarctic snow is too dry and powdery. That's why penguins don't have snowball fights.*

* It's one of the reasons. Also, they can't pick up snow with their flippers!

What's the matter?

When scientists study "stuff," they call it matter. Matter is everything: the air, the ocean, your hand, this book. It exists in different states depending on how it behaves. The three basic states that you will recognize are solid, liquid, and gas. Changes in state happen with a change in conditions: for example, when the temperature rises or falls. Water is a liquid but can become a solid (ice) when it is cooled and a gas when it is heated.

Liquids turn into solids when they reach their freezing point.

Spot the difference

It can be easy to see different states: ice looks totally different from water. But how do we describe them? Solids keep their shape at room temperature: a table does not change shape by itself. Liquids can flow and take the shape of their container. A pint of milk can be the shape of the bottle or carton, or a puddle on the counter. Gases are often invisible, but they float around to fill the space they are in.

Changing states

Water changes state quite easily. Other things need more extreme temperatures to change from one state to another. These temperatures are known as freezing point, melting point, and boiling point. Ice melts into water at 32°F (0°C). Lava is molten or melted rock, with a temperature between 1,292 and 2,192°F (700 and 1,200°C)!

Watery world

There is plenty of water on our planet. Most of it is in its liquid state, but salty: the oceans contain about 96.5 percent of all of Earth's water. A lot of it is frozen in icecaps and glaciers at the poles. It also exists as moisture in the ground. When this comes into contact with hot rocks, the water is heated enough to turn into steam. This can escape through the surface as geysers (giant spouts of boiling water and steam) and hot springs.

GALLIUM IS A METAL WITH SUCH A LOW MELTING POINT THAT IT GOES RUNNY IN YOUR HAND!

Did You Know

DIAMONDS CAN BURN

In 1772 a French scientist named Antoine Lavoisier used a giant magnifying glass to set fire to a diamond inside a glass jar. This experiment helped him find out all sorts of things about the chemical world.

A single substance

Lavoisier's experiment helped scientists with their discoveries about **elements**. An element is a pure substance that cannot be broken down into any other ingredients. Diamonds are made of the element carbon. When Lavoisier's diamond burned, it reacted with another element: oxygen. Together, the two elements formed a new substance: carbon dioxide gas.

LAVOISIER WAS EXECUTED IN 1794 DURING THE FRENCH REVOLUTION. A JUDGE SAID THAT FRANCE HAD "NO NEED FOR SCIENTISTS."

Charcoal and graphite (the "lead" in a pencil) are also pure carbon!

Tough as diamonds

Diamonds form deep below Earth's surface. They are crystals of pure carbon that have been squashed and heated over millions of years. They are carried closer to the surface by **magma** currents and dug out of the ground in diamond mines. Diamonds are the hardest substance we know, but because they are made of carbon (which is flammable) they will burn under the right conditions.

CARBON BONDS EXTREMELY WELL WITH OTHER ELEMENTS AND IS FOUND IN NEARLY 10 MILLION COMPOUNDS, OR CHEMICAL SUBSTANCES.

Building blocks?

All elements are made of tiny specks called **atoms**. They are so small, they cannot even be seen under a microscope. They are the simplest building blocks of the stuff around us: what scientists call matter. An element is pure because it is made of just one kind of atom. Carbon, oxygen, gold, hydrogen...they are each made of a different type of atom, that's why they are all unique.

A brief history of science

People in ancient times didn't know about elements. They thought that everything in nature was made up of air, fire, water, and earth. Alchemists tried to find a miracle potion that would make them live forever, or a way to turn common metals into precious gold. By the sixteenth century, many had left this magical approach behind, and a more modern science was born.

YOU ARE MADE OF STARDUST

Everything in the universe is made of chemical elements: you, your bed, the moon... EVERYTHING. It was all formed at the heart of a star, way back when the universe began. How mind-blowing is that?

Did You Know

Over half the human body is made up of water, or H_2O, containing hydrogen and oxygen.

Written in the stars

When the early universe expanded, particles quickly clumped together into atoms. The first, and simplest, were hydrogen atoms. These in turn joined to form helium, creating stars. Gradually, more and more elements were formed. Those elements are found today in your body: calcium in your bones, iron in your blood, and lots and lots of oxygen, carbon, and hydrogen.

So THAT'S what an atom looks like...

The number of electrons is different in every element.

It's a small world

Atoms are tiny, but they are made up of even tinier ingredients: **protons**, **neutrons**, and **electrons**. Protons and neutrons sit together in the middle, called the **nucleus**. Electrons spin around this nucleus like planets around a sun.

Light creates light

The nuclei of atoms join together to form new elements. This is called **fusion**. In space, gravity pulls together light elements and intense heat fuses them into heavier elements. So from the two lightest elements (hydrogen and helium) we get lithium, carbon, nitrogen...all the way up to iron.

Did You Know

Atoms are so small that if you lined up an atom for every person on Earth, they would only form a line about 3 ft (1 m) long.

Life story of a star

A star is a ball of elements, all fusing together and giving off light. A large star is hot enough to create some elements, but not all. When a star runs out of hydrogen it begins to collapse and get even hotter. This extra heat allows the creation of heavier elements. The dying star (called a supernova) pulses and eventually explodes, sending all of its elements out into space. Sometimes two dying stars may collide, producing all sorts of heavier elements.

TABLE SALT IS MADE OF TWO POISONS

Don't panic! It is still safe to sprinkle salt on your fries. Salt is a compound: a special chemical mix of different substances. When they bond together, the new substance can be completely different from the original ingredients.

Something new

Atoms are building blocks that can be joined together in different ways. Salt is made up of two types of atom: sodium and chlorine. Sodium is a silvery white metal and chlorine is a greenish gas, and both are extremely poisonous in some of their forms. However, they can be bonded together to form sodium chloride ($NaCl$), which is the white crystalline substance you use in cooking.

ALL ELEMENTS HAVE THEIR OWN CHEMICAL SYMBOL OF ONE OR TWO LETTERS.

SALT

Did You Know Your body needs salt to work properly. It contains about 9 oz (250g) of the stuff.

Mmm, that lovely swimming pool smell!

You can usually smell the chlorine in the water, but it is perfectly safe.

Safe water

Chlorine acts really well as a disinfectant to kill off germs. It can be added to water in tiny quantities to make it safe to swim in or drink. Most swimming pools and water companies prefer to use a powder or liquid that contains chlorine, instead of storing poisonous chlorine gas.

Crunching on crystals

Look carefully at table salt and you should see that it is made of tiny, regular cubes called **crystals**. They are formed when water evaporates, leaving the sodium and chlorine atoms which are bound together by electrical forces, or bonds.

Did You Know

Salt, sugar, ice, pencil lead, diamonds, and rubies are all crystals! (But they're not all edible, obviously.)

Sun, sea, and ... salt?

The metal sodium cannot be found in nature, although it occurs in large amounts in its other forms. It is easily found as NaCl in seawater. It also forms beautiful salt flats such as this one in Bolivia. When prehistoric lakes dried up, the salt was left behind, forming a white crust.

13

Did You Know

RAIN CAN DISSOLVE BUILDINGS

Pollution in the air contains many nasty substances. Some of these dissolve in the rain, and fall to Earth causing damage to buildings, forests, food crops, rivers, and wildlife.

Acid rain

Lots of human activity creates pollution. Chemicals escape into the air and mix with the gases in the atmosphere. They react to form sulfur dioxide and nitrogen oxides, which dissolve easily in water. This makes sulfuric acid and nitric acid. These fall to Earth as **acid rain**, dissolving soft rocks such as sandstone and limestone. The acid rain also gets into our rivers, killing off plants, fish, and other creatures that live there.

SNOW, SLEET, AND FOG CAN ALSO BECOME ACIDIC AND CAUSE DAMAGE.

Cars and other vehicles burn fossil fuels and create acid rain.

Spreading the damage

Polluting chemicals rise high into the sky and are blown by the wind. They travel vast distances, so many countries are affected, even if they try to reduce their own pollution levels. Once the acid rain gets into the water system, it flows through all our streams and rivers, reaching lakes and reservoirs.

Rain damage

Acid rain affects more than just our statues and buildings. It gets into the soil and stops trees growing. It kills off their leaves and needles, and makes them much more vulnerable to diseases, pests, and cold weather. It reduces crops of foods such as carrots and broccoli, and changes the soil so that some plants just won't grow.

VOLCANIC ERUPTIONS CAN CAUSE ACID RAIN, BUT MOST DAMAGE IS DONE BY HUMAN ACTIVITY.

Fossil fuels

Power stations are the main cause of acid rain. They burn **fossil fuels** (such as coal and gas) to generate electricity for us to use in our homes, schools, and offices. This releases large amounts of sulfur dioxide and nitrogen oxides. We need to find cleaner ways of making electricity, and to cut down on how much electricity we use, to help reduce acid rain.

POPCORN POPS WHEN WATER TURNS TO STEAM

Of all the different types of corn, only one will go POP! Even then, it needs the right conditions. The most important thing is that it contains the correct amount of water.

How popcorn pops

A kernel of corn is made up of a hard outer shell, with a starchy substance and a small amount of water inside it. At a hot enough temperature the water becomes steam. This makes it expand, so it breaks open the hard shell. The inside turns fluffy, the steam escapes, and you hear the characteristic POP!

A CORN KERNEL GROWS UP TO FIFTY TIMES BIGGER WHEN IT POPS.

Did You Know Fizzy candies react with your spit! The moisture dissolves the crystals and makes them fizz.

Coffee beans contain over 800 chemicals mixed together.

Getting bigger

Why does water expand when it turns to steam? Like so many things in chemistry, It all boils down (groan...) to molecules and matter. A **molecule** is a group of atoms bonded together. A water molecule contains two atoms of hydrogen (H) and one atom of oxygen (O), or H_2O. The molecules in a gas move more quickly than in a liquid, and they are more spread apart: they occupy more space.

Food for thought

All sorts of chemical processes take place in the kitchen. Baking powder releases bubbles of carbon dioxide gas, which makes cakes rise. Cooking meat breaks down the protein molecules, which makes it more tender. Boiling carbohydrates like pasta or rice makes the starch in them swell and soften. Toasting bread breaks down the chemicals and turns them into carbon, making it go brown. Who knew cooking was such a science!

In the mix

A simple food can be made up of many different chemicals. Food scientists can extract these chemicals and use them artificially to create different tastes. For example, the chemicals from citrus fruit skins can be added to food to make it taste like lemons. However, these chemicals don't dissolve in water, so they can't be used to make lemon drinks. Many chemists are employed by the food industry to figure out how these things work.

17

FLOUR CAN EXPLODE

Don't be scared of baking, though. It won't happen in your kitchen! However, under the correct conditions, a cloud of fine powder can cause an explosion.

DUST EXPLOSIONS ARE OFTEN USED FOR SPECIAL EFFECTS ON FILM AND TV.

A big bang

Explosions are chemical reactions that need the right ingredients before they can happen. Tiny particles in a confined space can react with oxygen from the air and produce a big bang. It doesn't happen all the time; they also need something hot to ignite them. This may be a flame or a spark, but could also be a hot part of a machine, friction (two things rubbing together), or static electricity.

Pack it in!

The reason flour dust burns is that the particles are so tiny. They have a large surface area compared to their overall **mass***. The surface of a substance is the part that burns, so more surface means more potential to catch fire. A tightly packed material has less surface area, so is less flammable.

*Mass is the amount of "stuff" in something. A bowling ball has more mass than a balloon the same size.

Death by dust

Flour isn't the only substance that is dangerous in dust form. Any fine powder will burn under the right conditions: spices, coal dust, powdered metal, and even sugar. In 2008, 14 people died in a sugar explosion in the US.

HIGHLY FLAMMABLE

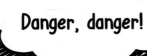

Danger, danger!

Ready to explode

A pile of flour won't burn, even if you hold a flame to it. Nor will a bag of flour. The tiny particles of flour have to be dispersed in the air, as they are in a container such as a storage silo. It can be a huge danger in industry, where storing and transporting powder can create the exact conditions needed for it to explode.

This is why you're told not to throw flour around when you're cooking...

THE PERIODIC TABLE BEGAN AS PLAYING CARDS

Scientists in the 1800s tried to arrange the elements in patterns according to their properties. In 1868 a Russian chemist playing Solitaire realized that cards with the elements written on them could be laid out in a similar way... and scientific history was made.

Looking for patterns

This Russian was Dmitri Mendeleev. He improved upon the work of chemists such as John Newlands, who had begun to arrange the elements starting with hydrogen (the lightest) as number 1. Mendeleev's card-game layout also took into account the elements' physical properties (what they look like, such as shiny solids) and chemical properties (for instance, how they react with other elements).

I'm taking a gamble on this theory...

THE ROWS IN MENDELEEV'S TABLE ARE CALLED PERIODS: THAT IS, REPEATING SETS OF LINKED ELEMENTS. THAT'S WHY WE CALL IT THE PERIODIC TABLE.

Dmitri Ivanovitch Mendeleev (1834–1907)

Rising numbers

The elements in the table are laid out according to their **atomic number.** This is the number of protons in the nucleus. Hydrogen appears first as it has just one; oxygen is further along as it has eight; iron (the "heavy" element formed in stars) has 26. Each element also has an atomic mass: the number of protons plus neutrons it contains. These increase as you move further down the table, too.

Solitaire and the periodic table use rows and columns. Ask Granny to show you!

Filling in the blanks

As Mendeleev arranged the elements, he realized that there were some gaps. Instead of rearranging them to fill the spaces, he made a great scientific leap. What if, he thought, we hadn't yet discovered all the elements? In fact, he even used their place in the table to predict what type of elements would fit in the holes. And he turned out to be right.

Are you sure?

Mendeleev was so convinced his theories were right that he questioned other scientific discoveries. He felt that there must be missing elements with predictable properties, and in 1875 a Frenchman, de Boisbaudran, discovered gallium, which seemed to fit one of the gaps. However, his measurements did not tally with Mendeleev's predictions. Mendeleev asked him to remeasure it, and the Frenchman found he had made a mistake!

Did You Know

Most of the elements on the periodic table are metals.

31
Ga
69.723

13
Al
26.982

THE WORLD IS RUNNING OUT OF HELIUM

Helium is the gas that is used to make balloons float. But there's bad news for birthdays, as it's in short supply! When helium is released into the atmosphere, it drifts off into space, never to return.

AT THE COLDEST TEMPERATURES, HELIUM BECOMES A LIQUID THAT CAN CLIMB UP THE WALLS OF CONTAINERS BY ITSELF!

Restricted resources

There are 118 elements in the periodic table, but not all of them are common, or easy to obtain. Helium is the second most abundant element in the universe, but is only produced on Earth by the breakdown of ancient rock, deep underground. The small amount of the gas that is trapped in the Earth's core must be carefully handled, as it is used for much more important things than party balloons.

Making it up

It sounds like nonsense, but not all of the 118 listed elements actually exist. That is: they can't be found naturally. Twenty of them (with atomic numbers 99 to 118) have only ever been made under laboratory conditions. Nine more were created artificially and helped fill the gaps in Mendeleev's table, but have since been found on Earth.

The name game

Many of the elements that were first discovered have descriptive names. Helium comes from the Greek *helios* which means "sun," as that is where it was first observed. Another gas, krypton, means "hidden," because it is almost undetectable. Later elements are often named after the scientist who discovered them, or the place where the scientist lived.

Divers often use helium in their scuba tanks.

THE TWENTY MAN-MADE ELEMENTS ARE CALLED SYNTHETIC ELEMENTS.

What else is helium used for?

Helium is extremely useful in medicine and scientific research. Liquid helium is so cold it can stop machinery from overheating. MRI scanners in hospitals use it, and so do superconducting magnets like the ones in the Large Hadron Collider at CERN in Switzerland. This is a giant underground tunnel where scientists recreate and study the conditions found at the beginning of the universe.

Endangered species

Scary newsflash: humans are using up the world's resources of precious elements. Several of these are known as Rare Earth Elements and are really hard to extract from the rocks where they are mined. But we are demanding them more and more, as they're vital ingredients in today's gadgets and technology, from headphones and hybrid cars to drugs and pacemakers.

WATER CAN MAKE THINGS EXPLODE

An element's place in the periodic table can give you a clue as to what it is like. Some are highly **reactive**, even with water. Potassium has to be stored in oil to keep it safe!

An explosive group

The elements in the first column (called group 1) of the periodic table are all known as alkali metals. Each of them reacts strongly with water and air; the lower down the group, the more reactive the metal is. Storing potassium in oil keeps it away from oxygen and water in the air. Further down the column we find rubidium, which explodes so violently in water that it can shatter its container!

Did You Know Potassium is a metal but is soft enough to cut with a knife.

Judging a book by its cover

You CAN judge an element by what's on the outside. Its electrons are arranged in circles, and the outer circle makes a big difference to how much an element reacts. Some elements have a neat, full set of electrons and are happy to stay that way: they are the least reactive. Others have gaps to fill, or spare electrons to get rid of, so they share or swap electrons with other elements. These ones are more reactive.

No reactions

At the opposite side of the table, in group 18, we find the **noble gases**. These have a full outer circle of electrons so are very unreactive. They include helium, neon, argon, and krypton, which can all be used to make decorative electric lights.

What shall I discover today?

Davy's discoveries

An extremely important English chemist named Humphry Davy discovered many of the group 1 and 2 metals. He was a big fan of **electrolysis**: passing electricity through liquids to separate them into different substances. He identified sodium, potassium, calcium, magnesium, boron, and barium using this method.

 Did You Know Your body needs potassium to stay healthy. It is found in potatoes, spinach, mushrooms, and bananas.

Sir Humphry Davy
(1778–1829)

25

BANANAS ARE RADIOACTIVE

These tasty fruits contain high levels of potassium, which your body needs, so that's a good thing. However, potassium atoms are unstable and decay (break down), making them radioactive.

What makes something radioactive?

Every element in the periodic table has a set number of protons. Potassium always has 19, and that's what makes it different from oxygen, or silver, or neon. Usually, the number of protons matches the number of neutrons, but sometimes an element can be unbalanced. It has different **isotopes**, containing more neutrons than protons. Some isotopes are unstable, with too much energy. This is released, and the element is said to be **radioactive**.

OTHER RADIOACTIVE FOODS INCLUDE BRAZIL NUTS, CARROTS, AND POTATOES.

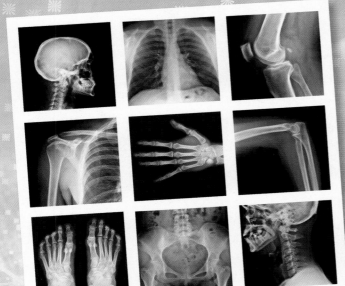

Radiation all around

Many radioactive elements are found in the natural world: in rocks, in water, and all around us in the stars and space. Scientists have learned how to make use of these elements for all sorts of helpful things. They are used in medicines, X-ray machines, smoke detectors, and to tell how old rocks and fossils are.

Danger! Danger!

High levels of radioactivity are dangerous to living creatures. The energy from the particles can pass through skin, and straight into the cells of the body. It damages the cells and causes radiation sickness. The body can't work properly anymore, and people become ill, or even die. People who work with radioactive substances wear protective clothing and limit the time they spend exposed to radiation.

This phone has me in peels of laughter.

Risky radiation

Bananas are safe to eat. They don't have high enough levels of radioactivity to do you any harm at all. You would have to eat millions and millions of bananas for the radioactivity to be dangerous. But a whole bunch of them just might contain enough radioactivity to register on a Geiger counter. That's a machine that counts how many radioactive particles are present. They show up on a screen, but also make a click. The faster the clicking, the more particles there are zooming around.

27

SALT CAN MAKE WATER SHRINK

If you slowly pour table salt into a full glass of water, the water level will go down! It's magic! Except of course it's not: it's science.

What's happening?

You would expect that adding salt would make the water rise and spill over the edge. Before that happens, though, scientific shenanigans take place. It's complicated, but the salt crystals have a charge that acts on the water molecules and pulls them closer together. That makes the water take up less space. As more salt is added, however, it begins to fill up the gaps between the water molecules, until eventually the space is taken up (known as saturation point) and the water overflows.

THE OCEANS ARE SLOWLY GETTING SALTIER AS RIVERS CARRY ROCK SALTS INTO THE SEA.

Mixing it up

Generally, salt water and freshwater mix quite easily. Try it: if you pour tap water into a glass of salty water it will mix together and taste less salty than the original. This usually happens when rivers flow into the sea. However, under certain circumstances, water does not mix so well. When the Rio Negro, with almost black water, meets the Amazon River in Brazil, the two rivers run side by side without mixing!

Different temperatures, speed, and density keep the two rivers separate.

A salty solution

Salt water and freshwater have some different properties. Salt water has different boiling and melting points from fresh water. Adding salt lowers the melting temperature, which is why we sprinkle salt onto ice to melt it.

Don't be dense

Salt water also has a greater density than freshwater. A bottle of salt water has more mass than the same sized bottle of freshwater. The salt water has more molecules, so it is denser. Objects float if they are less dense than their surrounding substance. That's (partly) how giant ocean liners work; their insides contain enough air to make them less dense than the water.

THE DEAD SEA IS SO SALTY IT IS VERY DENSE. PEOPLE CAN FLOAT WITHOUT TRYING!

CAT PEE GLOWS IN THE DARK

Freaky, huh? All urine, particularly cat urine, contains the element phosphorus, which glows yellowish-green when oxygen is present. It is even easier to see with a black light or ultraviolet light.

MUCH OF THE PHOSPHORUS ON EARTH WAS BROUGHT HERE BY METEORITES.

Way to glow

Black lights are the ones used in displays (at museums and theme parks) to make things glow and look spooky. They will make teeth and white clothes glow in the dark. In a dark room, these lights will pinpoint any puddles your pet cat might have left. Confusingly, some other substances are called "phosphorescent" because they glow, although they don't contain phosphorus!

TOO MUCH PHOSPHORUS IN RIVERS AND LAKES CAN CAUSE A BUILDUP OF ALGAE.

Strike a light

Phosphorus exists in two forms: red and white. It is used to make matches as it is very flammable (it catches fire easily). Old-fashioned "strike-anywhere" matches contain white phosphorus. They can be rubbed against a hard surface to cause friction, which heats the white phosphorus and makes it ignite. Safety matches are more common these days, as they won't accidentally catch fire in the box. Red phosphorus is mixed into the sandpaper on the matchbox, and the match only lights when it is struck against the sandpaper.

Cowboys lit "strike-anywhere" matches on the soles of their boots!

Playing with fire

Phosphorus was first discovered in 1669 by a German alchemist named Henning Brand. He collected urine (buckets and buckets of it, yuck!) so he could boil it and try to turn it into gold. Instead, he noticed that it glowed in the dark... and burst into flames! He named it from the words meaning "light-bearer" in Greek.

Spread it around

Phosphorus is extremely important. Our bodies need it for our bones, teeth, cells, and DNA. It combines with other chemicals to form phosphates, which are also vital for plant growth. Farmers use it in fertilizers. Today, most of it comes from rocks, but in the nineteenth century, it was collected in the form of guano (that's the dung of bats, seabirds, and seals). Guano is increasingly popular again these days, as an organic alternative to other fertilizers.

COLA DRINKS CAN BE USED TO CLEAN TOILETS

Cola rots your teeth if you drink too much of it. But can you put cola drinks to work? The same ingredients that cause tooth damage can be useful for cleaning bathroom grime!

Acid attack

Cola contains many ingredients, including three acids (carbonic, phosphoric, and citric). Acids can be weak or strong, with the strongest ones able to corrode (eat away at) all sorts of things. They can irritate or burn your skin and damage your tooth enamel, so you should limit how many soft drinks you have. The acids in cola will break down the dirt in a toilet bowl, leaving it shiny and clean when you flush!

IN THE MALDIVES ISLANDS, COLA IS MADE FROM SEAWATER WITH THE SALT REMOVED!

Hey, ladies, we're famous!

Bees use acidic stings to defend themselves.

Acids all around

Scientists use the pH scale to measure acidity. A neutral solution (like pure water) has a pH of 7. An acid has a pH value below 7. The closer it is to zero, the stronger it is. There are acids everywhere, without you even knowing it: milk contains lactic acid, tea contains tannic acid, and oranges and lemons contain citric acid.

On the inside

Our bodies contain various acids to help us function. One of them is found in your stomach: hydrochloric acid. It kills off harmful bacteria and helps to digest your food. It is so strong that your stomach has to produce a sticky mucus lining to prevent the acid eating the stomach walls! Your body also produces lactic acid when you exercise, and that's what can make your muscles ache.

The other end of the scale

Acids can be neutralized by bases or alkalis, which have a pH value above 7. They often feel slimy and soapy to touch. Bleach and caustic soda are strong bases that can burn your skin and hurt your eyes and throat. Weaker bases are used in toothpaste, antacid remedies, laundry detergent, and hair conditioner. Ocean water is weakly alkaline; it has a pH of around 8.

AN ALKALI IS A BASE THAT CAN BE DISSOLVED IN WATER.

THERE IS GOLD IN YOUR COMPUTER

Gold is an element that has some very useful qualities. It is used to make parts for computers and phones, although there isn't enough to make it worth pulling your old PC to pieces!

Simply the best

Electronic devices such as phones and computers need tiny metal parts called connectors that conduct (carry) electricity. Copper is a good, cheap conductor, but it doesn't carry electricity as fast as is needed inside a computer. Silver is the best conductor, but it reacts with air and moisture creating a thin layer of tarnish on the outside, which stops it from working properly. Gold is the best choice for the computer industry. It is a great conductor of electricity, and it is highly unreactive, so it doesn't tarnish or fall apart as it gets older.

THE CHEMICAL SYMBOL FOR GOLD IS AU. IT COMES FROM THE LATIN NAME FOR GOLD, WHICH IS AURUM.

Did You Know

There is more gold in 1 ton of PCs than in 17 tons of gold ore.

Gold is heavier than the other dirt, so it sinks to the bottom.

Panning for gold

Gold can be found in rocks; this is called gold ore. The ore is dug out of the ground at gold mines, and mixed with other chemicals to separate the metal from the rocks. Gold also occurs naturally in small lumps called nuggets, often in the sand and gravel in riverbeds. Gold prospectors use large, shallow pans to swirl the sand around and separate tiny bits of gold. Scientists think that most of the gold was brought to Earth from space by meteorites.

Did You Know

The oceans contain gold worth trillions of dollars, but it is too diluted to be worth trying to extract it.

Mega metal

Most metallic elements are shiny solids that conduct heat and electricity. Metals are also malleable: they can be hammered into new shapes without breaking. Gold is the most malleable of all metals. It can be beaten into thin sheets called gold leaf. A single gram can be flattened into a sheet the size of a (very, very thin) bath towel! It becomes see-through and is used as a coating inside space visors, to protect the astronaut from the sun's harmful rays.

Perfectly precious

Alchemists searched for ways to make gold from other substances, but why is it so special? It is rare, but it is also beautiful and useful. Its appearance, and its resistance to decay, led to its use on many precious artifacts. It was used to show power and wealth, and is still valued today as currency and for decorative items, as well as in the computer industry.

IF YOU CAN SMELL CABBAGE, BEWARE!

The world's smelliest substance is a gas called mercaptan. It stinks of rotting cabbage, leeks and garlic, or even dirty socks. But it can save your life!

Early warning

Natural gas is used in many buildings for cooking and heating. It is transported through pipelines and used for water heaters, ovens, and radiators. Natural gas is extremely flammable. A tiny little spark can ignite it and cause a huge explosion. It is hard to tell it is there, as it has no smell or taste. So gas companies add tiny amounts of super smelly mercaptan, which acts as a warning if the gas is leaking into the air around us.

MERCAPTAN IS SO SMELLY THAT YOUR NOSE CAN SENSE ONE PARTICLE OUT OF A BILLION AIR PARTICLES!

Gas workers look for vultures to guide them to leaking pipes.

What a whiff

Mercaptan gas gives an unpleasant aroma to many things. It's what makes a person's breath smell, and the nasty gases they release from elsewhere! It is found in some nuts and cheeses and is also present in our blood and brains. Dead, decaying animals give off mercaptan gas. Scavengers such as the turkey vulture pick up on the smell to guide them to their next meal, and they have been seen circling overhead if there is a gas leak!

SMELLY MERCAPTAN GASES FROM A LEAK IN A FRENCH CHEMICAL FACTORY SPREAD THE AWFUL STENCH FOR OVER 200 MILES!

Filling the space

All gases have certain things in common. Their particles are full of energy and are free to flow in any direction they want. They spread out to fill whatever container they are kept in. You can see this in a balloon filled with air; no matter what shape you twist the balloon into, the air molecules still spread out through the whole balloon.

Changing state

Cooling natural gas changes it from a gas into a liquid. Its molecules slow down and take up less space. Natural gas can be stored at very low temperatures as LNG (liquefied natural gas) and transported in tankers instead of along pipelines.

37

DYNAMITE WAS FIRST CALLED "SAFETY POWDER"

Dynamite was invented in 1867 by the great scientist Alfred Nobel. It was intended to make it safer to blow up rocks for mining and building.

Boom-time

The nineteenth century was a time of exploration, invention, and development. People needed controlled explosions to blast rocks into pieces for building materials, or to make way for canals and train tracks. They often used gunpowder, but it was dangerous and not very strong. The other option was nitroglycerine, invented in 1847. The problem was, it was uncontrollably dangerous. Even a tiny jolt could make it explode, either while it was being transported or while the miners were putting it into the rocks.

ALFRED NOBEL HAD PATENTS FOR 355 OF HIS INVENTIONS AND IDEAS.

Did You Know

Dynamite has the same ingredient as cat litter.

Old dynamite leaks; the ingredients seep out and make it much more dangerous than new dynamite.

A safe solution

Alfred Nobel's family owned a nitroglycerine business, where his younger brother Emil was killed in a factory explosion. Alfred worked for years to find a way to make nitroglycerine safer to use. His solution was dynamite, which mixed nitroglycerine with diatomite (a kind of earth) that stopped it exploding by mistake. The dynamite was packaged in sticks, with a fuse to light them from a safe distance.

Making peace

Unfortunately for Alfred, his invention could also be used for violence and killing. When his brother Ludvig died in 1888, a newspaper mistakenly reported it as Alfred's death, and nicknamed him "The Merchant of Death." Alfred was devastated to read this and swore to change his reputation. He decided to use his huge fortune to set up a prize fund for other great scientists. Nowadays, his name is remembered most in connection with the Nobel Peace Prize.

I just want a peaceful life...

Alfred Nobel
(1833–1896)

PLAY-DOH WAS INVENTED TO CLEAN WALLPAPER!

Some of the best scientific discoveries happen by accident, while searching for a solution to a completely different problem. Play-Doh started life as a cleaning product!

PLAY-DOH IS MADE OF FLOUR, SALT, OIL, WATER, AND A WEAK ACID CALLED BORIC ACID.

Lateral thinking

In the 1930s, homeowners struggled to keep their walls clean. Their coal-burning fires left soot everywhere, and they used a white dough-like substance to clean it off. Unfortunately for the company that made this dough, the switch to cleaner fuels meant that their product was no longer needed. Cue one bright idea: add dye, give it a new name, and sell it to schools as clay for model making!

A sticky situation

Scientists seem to struggle with sticky stuff. Some glue is too sticky, some is just not sticky enough. But add a creative mind, and you can find a use for either. Post-it notes were invented in 1968 when Doctor Spencer Silver was struggling to find an extra strong glue. Instead, he invented a less sticky glue that is ideal for attaching pieces of paper and peeling them off again.

By contrast, scientists in World War II were trying to find a clear plastic to make gun sights, but had problems because their product was too sticky. They were working with cyanoacrylate but it stuck to everything it touched! It took years for them to realize its potential as a "super glue," but now it is used for everything from mending mugs to fixing Formula One cars.

SUPERGLUE IS STRONG ENOUGH TO HOLD PARTS OF FORMULA ONE CARS TOGETHER, EVEN AT 200 MILES PER HOUR!

Sticky buns don't stick to Teflon!

A nonsticky situation

Teflon is the ultimate nonstick substance, used for baking sheets, cooking pans, and even hard-wearing clothes. Guess what? It was also discovered by accident, during an unrelated experiment!

Did You Know

CHOCOLATE IS POISONOUS TO DOGS

Chocolate contains a chemical compound called theobromine. It is similar to caffeine, the chemical found in coffee and cola, and can be deadly if a dog eats it.

Out of reach

Chocolate and caffeine are alkaloids. They contain nitrogen molecules and are commonly found in nature. Like all poisons, the bigger the dose, the more dangerous it is. Dark chocolate contains more theobromine than milk chocolate, so is worse for a dog. A small dog will be badly affected by a small dose; even a chocolate chip cookie could cause problems. To play it safe, hide your treats from hungry pets!

Please? I would share my dog food with you.

A poison dart frog's bright skin is a warning that it is toxic.

Plants on prescription

Alkaloids are found in around one fifth of all plants. Poppies, tulips, lily of the valley, and daffodils contain them, as do the seeds of apples, cherries, and apricots. Each contains only a tiny amount, but it is best not to eat them! Throughout history, people have found how to use these poisons to their benefit. Some, like nicotine, are put in pesticides to kill insects. Morphine and codeine are ingredients in painkillers. Quinine was once the main treatment for the deadly disease malaria.

Poison arrows

Certain South American plants contain alkaloids that can be mixed to make curare. This is a deadly substance loaded onto arrow tips and blowgun darts. Once it enters the victim's blood it shuts down their system until they can no longer breathe. Some frogs secrete alkaloid toxins through their skin, giving them the nickname of poison dart frogs.

FOXGLOVE PLANTS CAN BE USED AS HEART MEDICINE, BUT WILL KILL YOU IN THE WRONG DOSE!

Fighting back

Snakes and spiders bite thousands of people every year, and some have a venom that can kill. Luckily, doctors can treat poisonous bites with an antivenom. Scientists collect the deadly venom and inject tiny doses of it into other animals, which build up an immunity in their blood. This blood can be gathered and used to treat people who have been bitten.

Did You Know

SOME CARS CAN RUN ON HUMAN POOP!

The world is running out of fossil fuels such as oil, coal, and gas. Scientists need to find other ways to supply energy for cars, homes, and factories.

A dirty business

Fossil fuels are a limited resource. Once we use them all up, there is no way of making any more. That's not the only problem: when we burn these fuels, they create pollution and release greenhouse gases. These gases upset the balance of Earth's atmosphere, which in the long term will have a damaging effect on life on this planet. But what alternatives are there?

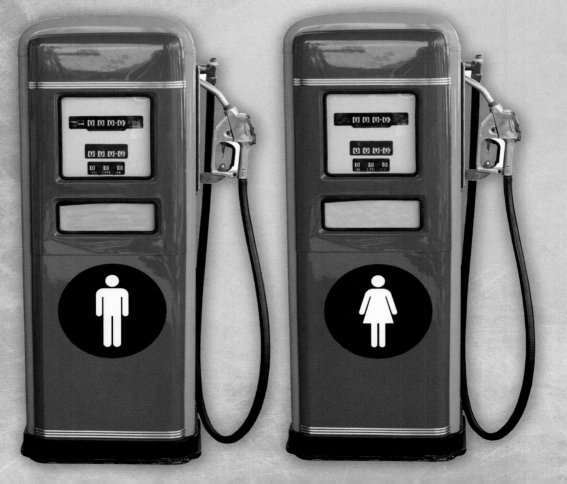

44

Biofuels

Cars and buses can be made to run on **biofuels**. Usually, these are made from plants, such as sugarcane, corn, and vegetable oil. They produce fewer harmful chemicals when they burn. However, they require large amounts of crops, which take up a lot of farming land and water for irrigation. Some people argue that it would be better to invest this effort and money into producing food, not fuel.

Cleaning up

One solution is to reuse waste products. Scientists have figured out how to convert human sewage and food waste into fuel. It is cheaper than converting crops into fuel, and recycles a product that nobody wants! Bacteria is added to the sewage to break it down and produce gas, which can be used for cooking and heating, as well as to power vehicles.

When you flush the toilet, the waste goes to a sewage treatment plant.

HENRY FORD'S EARLY CAR DESIGNS WERE INTENDED TO RUN ON PLANT-BASED FUEL.

Maybe I can help?

Waste wanted

It's not only human waste that has potential as fuel. Plant waste, such as corncobs and stalks, can be turned into ethanol but it is a tricky process. Scientists have found that pandas have just the right bacteria for breaking down tough plant waste. Further studies could help us solve our fuel problems... and help to save an endangered species, too.

Glossary

acid rain Rainfall that contains sulfuric acid and nitric acid, caused by air pollution.

atomic number The number of protons in the nucleus of an element.

atoms The tiny particles that make up elements.

biofuel A fuel that comes from renewable plant or animal matter.

combustion A chemical reaction that involves the combination of fuel and oxygen to give off heat and light.

compound A substance formed when two or more elements react chemically with each other.

corrosion A chemical reaction that gradually destroys materials such as metals as they react with the oxygen in the surrounding air.

crystal A solid in which the atoms are arranged in regular geometrical shapes.

electrolysis Passing electricity through liquids to separate them into different substances.

electrons The tiny (subatomic) particles that make up atoms with a negative electrical charge. They spin around the nucleus of an atom.

element A chemical substance that cannot be broken down into any simpler substance.

fossil fuel A fuel such as coal or gas that has been formed over millions of years from the remains of animals and plants.

fusion When the nuclei of atoms join together to form new elements.

isotopes Atoms in an element that have different numbers of neutrons and protons.

magma Molten rock.

mass The amount of matter in an object.

molecule A group of atoms bonded together.

neutrons The tiny (subatomic) particles that make up atoms with no electrical charge.

noble gases A group of gases that are very unreactive (inert).

nucleus The central core of an atom made up of protons and neutrons.

patination A green film that forms on the surface of copper and bronze as they react with air.

periodic table A table of the chemical elements arranged in order of atomic number.

protons The tiny (subatomic) particles that make up atoms with a positive electrical charge.

radioactive Describes the property of some unstable elements (such as isotopes) to emit high-energy particles.

reactive In chemistry, the rate at which a substance tends to take part in chemical reactions.

Further Information: Websites

pbskids.org/zoom/games/kitchenchemistry/index.html
Kitchen chemistry challenges – choose from the virtual kitchen or the reality kitchen.

www.acs.org/content/acs/en/education/whatischemistry/adventures-in-chemistry.html
American Chemical Society website with facts, experiments, games, and much more.

www.chem4kids.com
A great website for basic information about all kinds of chemistry.

http://www.rsc.org/periodic-table
The Royal Society of Chemistry website hosts an interactive periodic table, with facts about the properties and history of each element, as well as the history of the periodic table itself.

www.sciencekids.co.nz/chemistry.html
A fun website with chemistry facts, quizzes, games, experiments, videos, and images.

Publisher's note to educators and parents: Our editors have carefully reviewed these websites to ensure that they are suitable for students. Many websites change frequently, however, and we cannot guarantee that a site's future contents will continue to meet our high standards of quality and educational value. Be advised that students should be closely supervised whenever they access the Internet.

Further Information: Books

A Beginner's Guide to the Periodic Table by Gill Arbuthnot (A&C Black, 2014)

Big Questions: It's Elementary! Putting the Crackle into Chemistry by Robert Winston (Dorling Kindersley, 2010)

Molecules: The Elements and Architecture of Everything by Nick Mann and Theodore Gray (Black Dog and Leventhal, 2014)

The Elements: A Visual Exploration of Every Known Atom in the Universe by Nick Mann and Theodore Gray (Black Dog and Leventhal, 2011)

What's Chemistry All About? by Alex Frith and Lisa Gillespie (Usborne, 2012)

Index